BASIC TECHNIQUES

FOLDING TERMS AND SYMBOLS

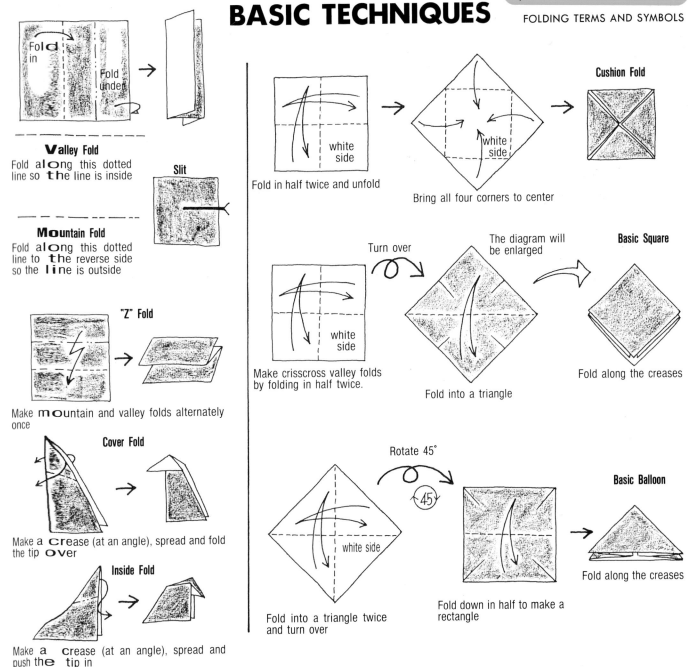

Valley Fold
Fold along this dotted line so the line is inside

Mountain Fold
Fold along this dotted line to the reverse side so the line is outside

Slit

"Z" Fold
Make mountain and valley folds alternately once

Cover Fold
Make a crease (at an angle), spread and fold the tip over

Inside Fold
Make a crease (at an angle), spread and push the tip in

Fold in half twice and unfold — white side

Cushion Fold
Bring all four corners to center — white side

Turn over

Make crisscross valley folds by folding in half twice. — white side

The diagram will be enlarged

Fold into a triangle

Basic Square
Fold along the creases

Rotate 45°

Fold into a triangle twice and turn over — white side

Fold down in half to make a rectangle

Basic Balloon
Fold along the creases

●PREFACE●

A single sheet of paper can be turned into any imaginative figure even by a small child. This is the charm of origami. It has developed children's creativity and dexterity for generations. There have been numerous traditional origami models, some of which are not seen any more. It is surprising that those centuries-old models often represent the most distinctive forms we can think of nowadays. In this book I introduce traditional models with a little twist to show them off, along with new creations. I hope you will share the joy of origami, doing it your way, or possibly creating innovative designs.

REIKO ASOU has studied children's education in Tokyo and while being a kindergarten teacher she began studying art in various media including research in traditional origami. In 1991, she became an origami instructor for Japan Origami Hall, since then she has been presiding over "Himawari", an origami circle, endeavoring to popularize the craft. She contributes much to cultural exchange not only in Japan but internationally.

ADORABLE ANIMALS

Animals always never fail to please small children. They will love making popular figures on their own and will be proud of themselves. Attach dots (use stickers) to make the features.

USE AS A HAND PUPPET

Body models are made separately to support the hand puppets.

RACCOON: see page 9 for head.
FOX: see page 9 for head.
CAT: see page 5 for head.

ELEPHANT: see page 9 for head.
RABBIT: see page 8 for head.
PIG: see page 5 for head.
For Body: see page 4.

①CAT

③RABBIT

⑤FOX

REVERSE SIDE (Note the different tails)

②PIG

⑥ELEPHANT

④RACCOON

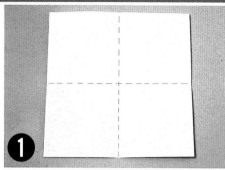

1 Fold in half twice. Unfold.

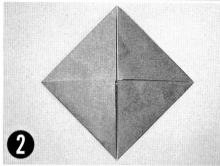

2 Bring all four corners to the center.

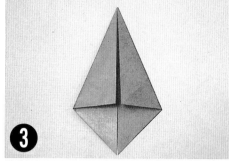

3 Fold two upper edges to align with the center.

4 Turn over and fold the bottom corner up to match the top corner.

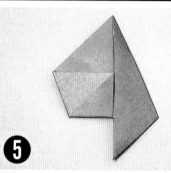

5 Pulling down the square corner, fold in the side to align with the center.

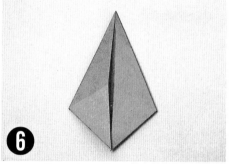

6 Repeat on the other side.

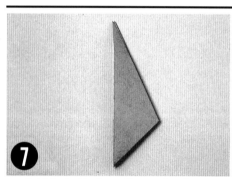

7 Fold in half along the center line.

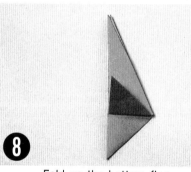

8 Fold up the bottom flap.

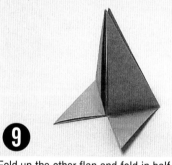

9 Fold up the other flap and fold in half along the center line. Unfold and stand by opening at 90°.

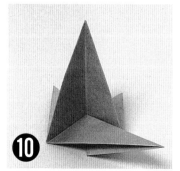

10 Fold down the inner triangle. (This is a reverse view)

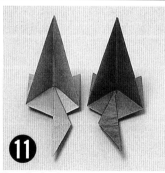

11 For **elephant** or **cat**, make a thin tail by folding to the center.

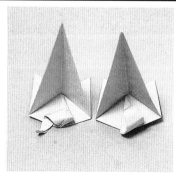

For **pig** or **rabbit**, make a curl on the thin tail.

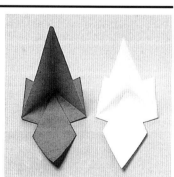

For **fox** and **raccoon**, fold symmetrically by inserting your finger and pressing down.

4

CAT

Use 5"×5" paper

1 Fold in half to make a triangle.

2 Fold side points to the bottom corner.

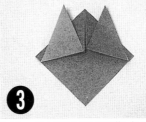

3 Fold up the flaps diagonally, leaving a little space from the side points.

4 Turn over and fold up the upper flap to match the top point.

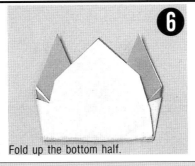

5 Turn over again and fold the sides in.

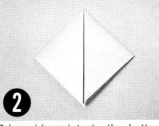

6 Fold up the bottom half.

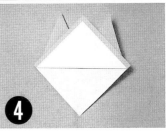

7 Fold top and bottom corners under to shape face.

PIG

Use 5"×5" paper

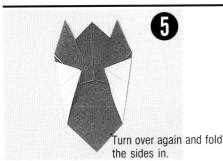

1 Begin with white side up. Fold in half to make a triangle.

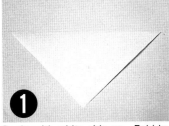

2 Bring side points to the bottom corner.

3 Fold up flaps diagonally, leaving a little space from the side points.

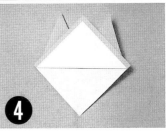

4 Turn over and fold up the upper flap leaving a little space from the side points.

5 Fold back the tip to match the fold.

6 Fold the tip under, in half.

7 Fold down flap and fold in the sides diagonally.

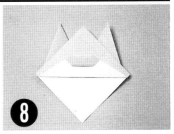

8 Return the folded flap to the former position.

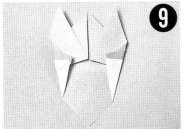

9 Turn over again and fold sides in.

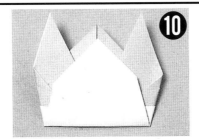

10 Fold up the bottom.

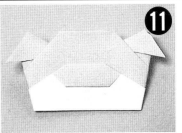

11 Turn over. Fold the top corner under. Fold down ears.

7 CICADA

Use unwoven fabric origami to represent transparency of the wings
Use 6" × 6" paper

1 Fold in half to make a triangle.

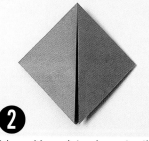

2 Bring side points down to the bottom corner.

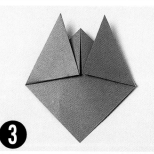

3 Fold up flaps diagonally from the side corners.

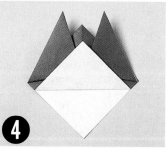

4 Fold up one lower flap to a point just short of the center.

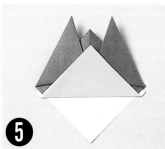

5 If using fabric origami, insert one quarter of another sheet of paper to line the upper flap.

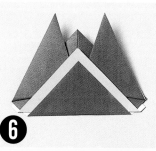

6 Fold up bottom flap, a little short of the center, to show the color contrast.

7 Rotate to make ½ turn. Turn over. Bring sides overlapping at the center.

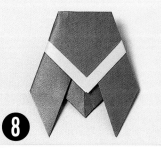

8 Turn over for completed cicada.

8 DRAGONFLY

Use 6"×6" paper

1 Make a diamond referring to steps ①-⑤ on page 48.

2 With the slitted end towards you, fold the lower sides in. Turn over and repeat.

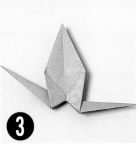

3 Bring up points (see inside fold on page 1), one at right angle, the other slightly upward.

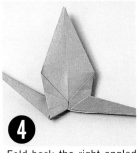

4 Fold back the right angled leg along its center crease.

5 Fold down one wing. Pull down the center triangle.

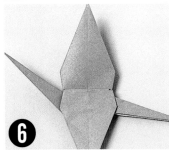

6 Insert the center triangle between wings.

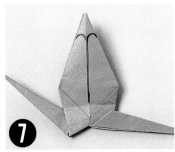

7 Bring the wing back and trim the tips.

8 Open the head part and roll in. Glue to secure.

9 Spread out the wings for completed dragonfly.

7

1 Fold in half to make a triangle.

2 Bring side points down to the bottom corner.

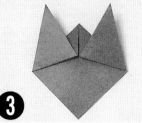

3 Fold up flaps diagonally from the side corners.

4 Turn over and fold up one flap to match the upper half.

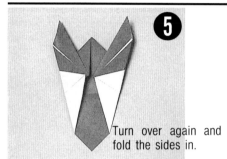

5 Turn over again and fold the sides in.

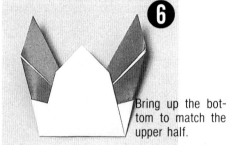

6 Bring up the bottom to match the upper half.

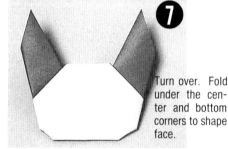

7 Turn over. Fold under the center and bottom corners to shape face.

1 Fold in half to make a triangle.

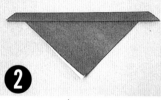

2 Fold down ½" from the top.

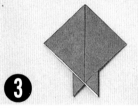

3 Bring top edges down to align at the center.

4 Fold them up in half.

5 Fold back upper flaps diagonally.

6 Fold down the triangles on the tips in half, and glue to secure.

7 Turn over and fold up one flap along the center.

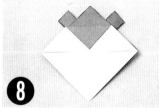

8 Fold back the tip to match the fold.

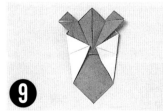

9 Turn over and fold the sides in.

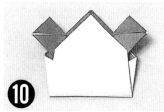

10 Fold up the lower half.

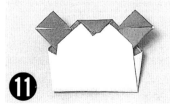

11 Fold down the center corner and glue to secure.

12 Turn over for completed raccoon.

ELEPHANT

❶

Fold in half to make a triangle.

❷

Divide the angle of the top corner into three.

❸

Fold along the dividing creases.

❹

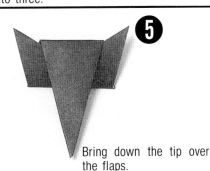

Fold up lower flaps along the bottom of triangle.

❺

Bring down the tip over the flaps.

❻

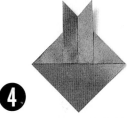

Make valley fold, then mountain fold to make trunk. Fold under the bottom corners.

FOX

❶

Fold in half to make a triangle.

❷

Fold down $\frac{1}{2}$" from the top.

❸

Bring top edges down to align at the center.

❹

Fold them up in half.

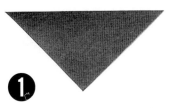

❺

Fold back the upper halves of the flaps diagonally.

❻

Turn over and fold up one flap along the center.

❼

Fold back the tip slightly over the center crease.

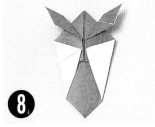

❽

Turn over and fold the sides in, tapering towards the bottom.

❾

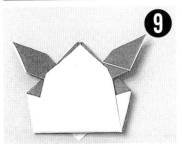

Fold up the bottom half.

❿

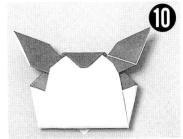

Fold down the center corner and glue to secure.

⓫

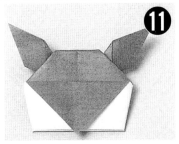

Turn over for completed fox.

9

⑨ GOLDFISH BALLOON

For instructions, see page 12.

LET'S GO FISHING!

Attach a paper clip to the mouth of the fish. Scatter several fish, hang a magnet from a stick and pretend you are fishing.

10 RABBIT BALLOON

For instructions, see page 12.

For instructions, see page 13.

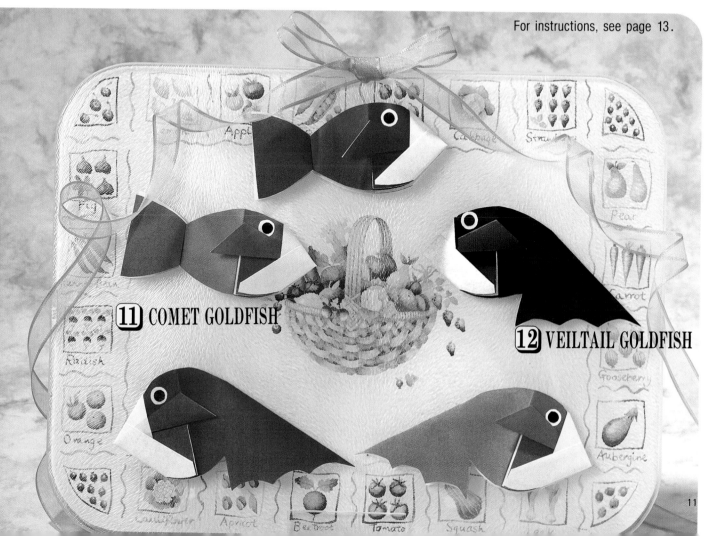

11 COMET GOLDFISH

12 VEILTAIL GOLDFISH

GOLDFISH BALLOON

1 Begin with colored side up. Fold in half and unfold; repeat to make valley folds crosswise. Turn over. Fold and unfold twice diagonally.

2 Press down using the creases.

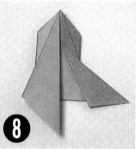

3 Fold up lower edges to meet at the center.

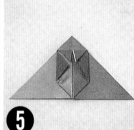

4 Fold side corners to the center.

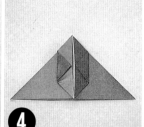

5 Fold upper flaps down, aligning the edges.

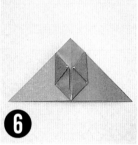

6 Fold down again and tuck the corners into the pockets.

7 Turn over and bring upper edges down to meet at the center.

8 Fold back one flap diagonally.

9 Bring up both sides and hold together. This makes the fin.

10 Blow into the opening for completed goldfish balloon.

RABBIT BALLOON

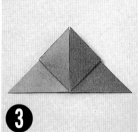

7 For steps ① – ⑥, refer to GOLDFISH BALLOON (this page). Turn over.

8 Bring up the bottom edges to meet at the center.

9 Fold back diagonally to form ears.

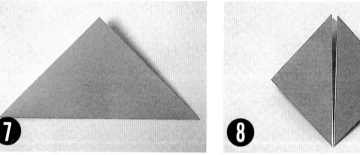

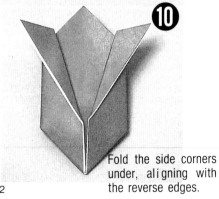

10 Fold the side corners under, aligning with the reverse edges.

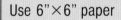

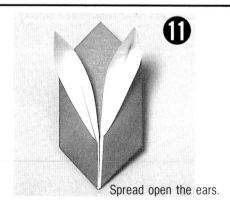

11 Spread open the ears.

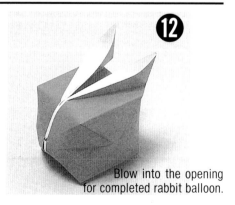

12 Blow into the opening for completed rabbit balloon.

For either model, steps ①-⑥ stay the same.

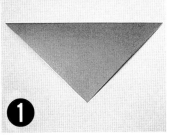

1 Fold in half to make a triangle.

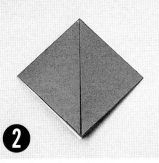

2 Bring down top edges to align at the center.

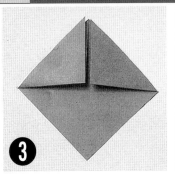

3 Fold up flaps in half.

4 Fold back diagonally.

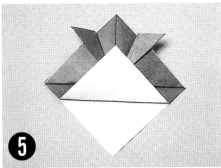

5 Fold up one flap so the corner reaches the middle of the upper triangle.

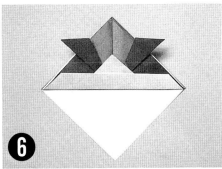

6 Fold up the rest along the center.

COMET

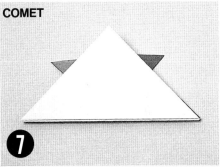

7 Turn over and fold up the lower triangle aligning edges.

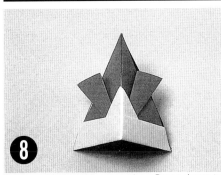

8 Open and bring sides together. Press down to fold.

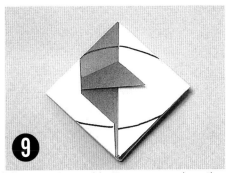

9 Trim away top and bottom corners along the lines.

10 Flip the white section to the right to make tail for completed comet.

VEILTAIL

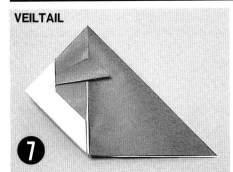

7 Do the same from ①-⑥. Open and bring the opposite corners together; press down to fold.

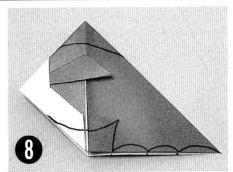

8 Trim along the lines.

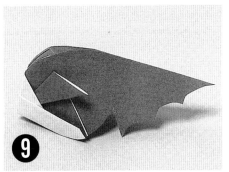

9 Completed veiltail.

13

⑬ HAMSTER

Special origami sheets with colored corners are used to make these models
Use 6"×6" paper

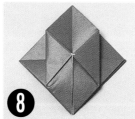

❼ For steps ①-⑥ refer to page 12. Flip to the left. Fold the triangle on the right in half. Fold down the flap along the middle.

❽ Flip the folds to the other side and fold the other triangle the same.

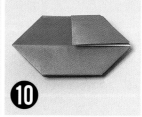

❾ Turn over and fold sides in to meet at the center.

❿ Flip both sides and rotate to make ¼ turn.

⓫ Fold back center corner into a triangle.

⓬ Unfold and turn under, using the crease just formed. Turn over and repeat.

⓭ Make ears by folding "Z" fold pleat on both sides.

⓮ Flip again and rotate to make ¼ turn.

⓯ Make sure the flaps with ears come underneath. Fold back sides a little inside so the corners stick out to make feet.

⓰ Glue back together so the ears come to the top. Blow into the opening for completed hamster.

x

14

14 PUPPY

For instructions,
see page 16.

15 KOALA BEAR

For instructions, see page 17.

15

HEAD

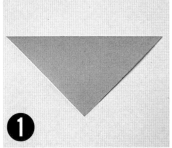

① Fold in half to make a triangle.

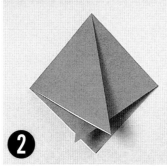

② Fold down upper edges to overlap at the center.

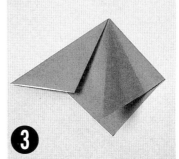

③ Divide the bottom of each flap into three, and fold back to make ear.

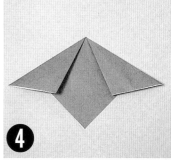

④ Repeat on the other side.

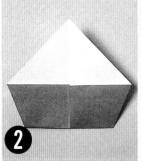

⑤ Fold back the tips.

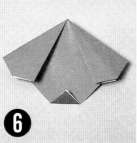

⑥ Unfold and fold inside, using the creases just formed. Fold up the bottom corner to make nose.

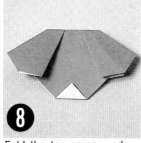

⑦ Tuck in the colored tip.

⑧ Fold the top corner under for completed head.

BODY

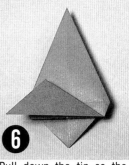

① Fold in half to make a triangle. Unfold and fold two edges to align at the center.

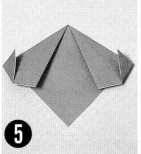

② Turn over and fold in half.

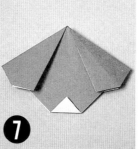

③ Lift center corner and pull down until the side aligns with the center. Press down to fold.

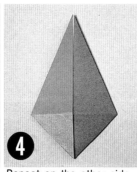

④ Repeat on the other side.

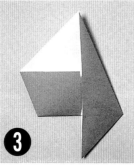

⑤ Bring down the tip to spread open. Fold up again, $\frac{1}{2}$" lower than former position.

⑥ Pull down the tip so the right edge aligns with the fold.

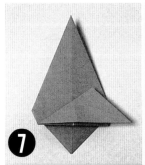

⑦ Unfold and repeat, folding to the other direction.

⑧ Unfold and make tail using the creases just formed.

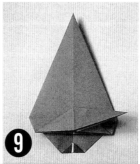

⑨ Fold up bottom corner a little.

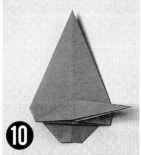

⑩ Unfold and fold under using the crease just formed.

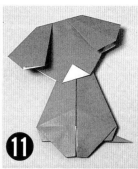

⑪ Turn over and join the head for completed puppy.

KOALA BEAR

Use 4"×4" paper for head, 6"×6" paper for body

HEAD

1 Begin with colored side up. Fold in half into a triangle. Bring upper edges to center.

2 Divide upper edge into quarters. Fold in side corners at one quarter.

3 Divide the center into three. Fold up one flap at one third from the top diagonally.

4 Fold the other flap the same.

5 Turn over. Fold up bottom corner to reach the center. Fold back its tip.

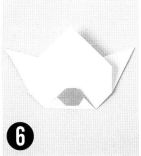

6 Fold down upper flap a little. Unfold the lower flap and fold under, using crease.

7 Fold in bottom corners to smooth out the face line.

8 Unfold. Lifting nose, press the sides using the creases to make vertical folds. Fold under the top corner.

9 Fold under the corners of nose. Trim ears along the lines.

10 Completed koala bear.

BODY

1 Begin with colored side up. Bring all corners to the center (cushion fold).

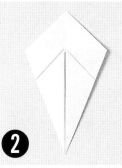

2 Turn over and fold lower edges to align with the center.

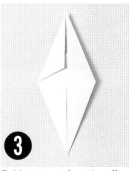

3 Fold upper edges to align with the center.

4 Turn over and open all flaps.

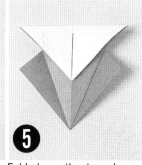

5 Fold down the top along the line connecting the side corners.

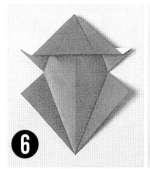

6 Fold back, leaving 3/8" from the crease just formed.

7 Fold in upper sides a little, pressing the lower section to align with shoulder edges.

8 Fold up bottom corner to align with the shoulder line.

9 Valley fold in half.

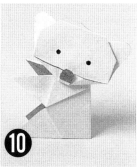

10 Join the head for completed koala bear.

16 FUR SEAL

For instructions, see page 20.

17 SEA OTTER

For instructions, see page 20.

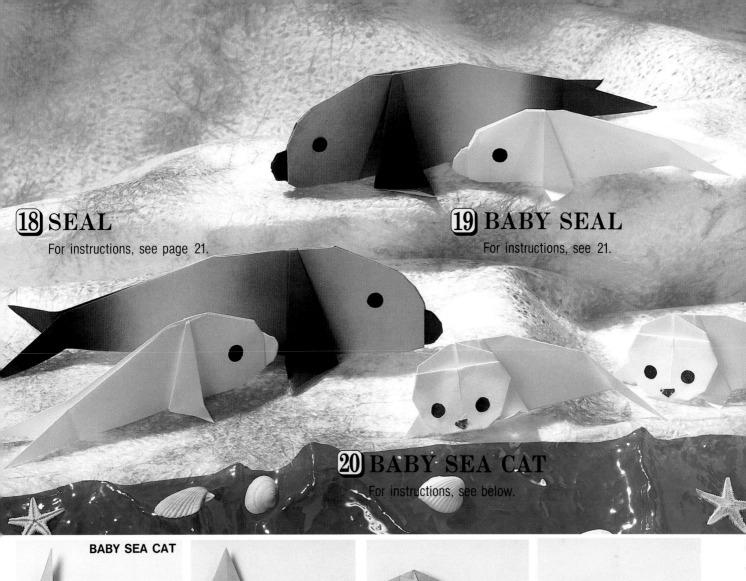

⑱ SEAL

For instructions, see page 21.

⑲ BABY SEAL

For instructions, see 21.

⑳ BABY SEA CAT

For instructions, see below.

BABY SEA CAT

7

For steps ① - ⑥, refer to page 20, but folding only one flipper. Make inside fold to form neck: pull up the left tip folding inside in half, and press down to stand upright.

8

Flip the center flap to the right and fold back to align with the center.   Open the head.

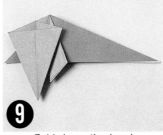

9

Fold down the head.

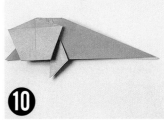

10

Fold the tip under to align with the bottom. Fold top corners inside to smooth out the back.

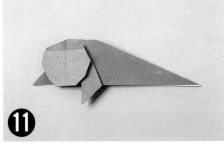

11

Fold under all corners to make round-shaped head.

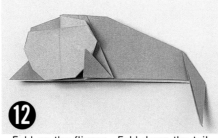

12

Fold up the flipper. Fold down the tail.

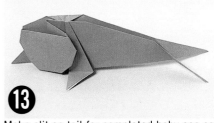

13

Make slit on tail for completed baby sea cat.

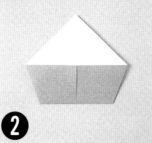

①

Fold in half into a triangle and unfold. Bring lower edges to the center crease.

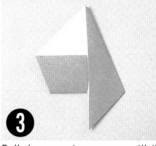

②

Mountain fold in half.

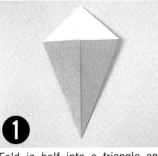

③

Pull down center corner until the side align with the center. Press down to fold.

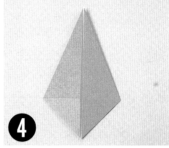

④

Repeat on the other side.

⑤

Bring down the tip to spread open.

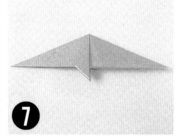

⑥

Fold in half lengthwise and rotate to make ¼ turn.

⑦

Fold center flap to align with the center. Repeat on the reverse side.

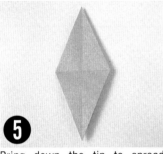

⑧

Make inside fold to form neck. Pull up the left tip folding inside in half, and press down to stand upright.

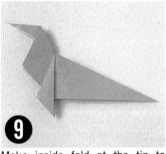

⑨

Make inside fold at the tip to make head.

⑩

Make a small inside fold again and tuck in.

⑪

Make 1½" slit at tail.

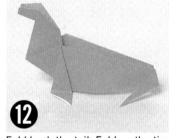

⑫

Fold back the tail. Fold up the tips of flippers to stand.

⑧

For steps ① - ⑥, refer to FUR SEAL(above). Rotate to make ½ turn. Fold tips to make head and flipper.

⑨

Make "Z" fold on the head.

⑩

Unfold. Tuck in the tip and push in, redoing the "Z" fold using the creases.

⑪

Make 2" slit on tail and fold inside.

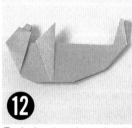

⑫

Tuck in the tips of tail. Fold bottom corners inside to stand.

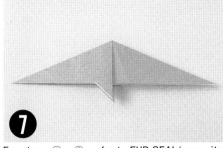

7

For steps ① - ⑥, refer to FUR SEAL(opposite page). Flip the center flap to the other side.

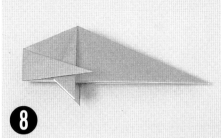

8

Repeat on the reverse side. Fold ⅓ from the right tip.

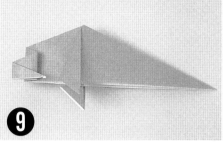

9

Make "Z" fold to make head.

10

Unfold and fold inside using the creases just formed.

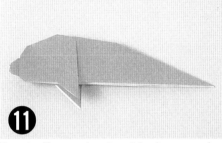

11

Round off nose, head and back corners by folding inside.

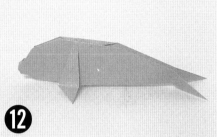

12

Make 1⅜" slit on tail and fold one back. Fold flippers to stand.

6

For steps ① - ⑤, refer to FUR SEAL. Fold lengthwise in half. Fold center flap towards left.

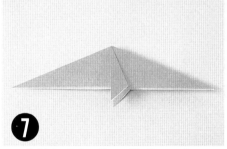

7

Fold back to align with the center.

8

Turn over and repeat. Fold back left point.

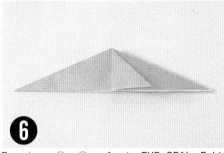

9

Make "Z" fold to form head.

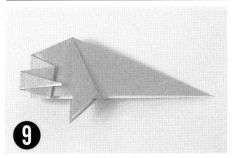

10

Unfold and fold again each crease to the other way.

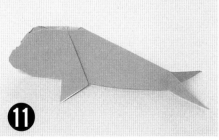

11

Round off nose, face, and back corners by folding inside.

Flick the tail upwards with your finger, and the horse will somersault and land on their feet.

22

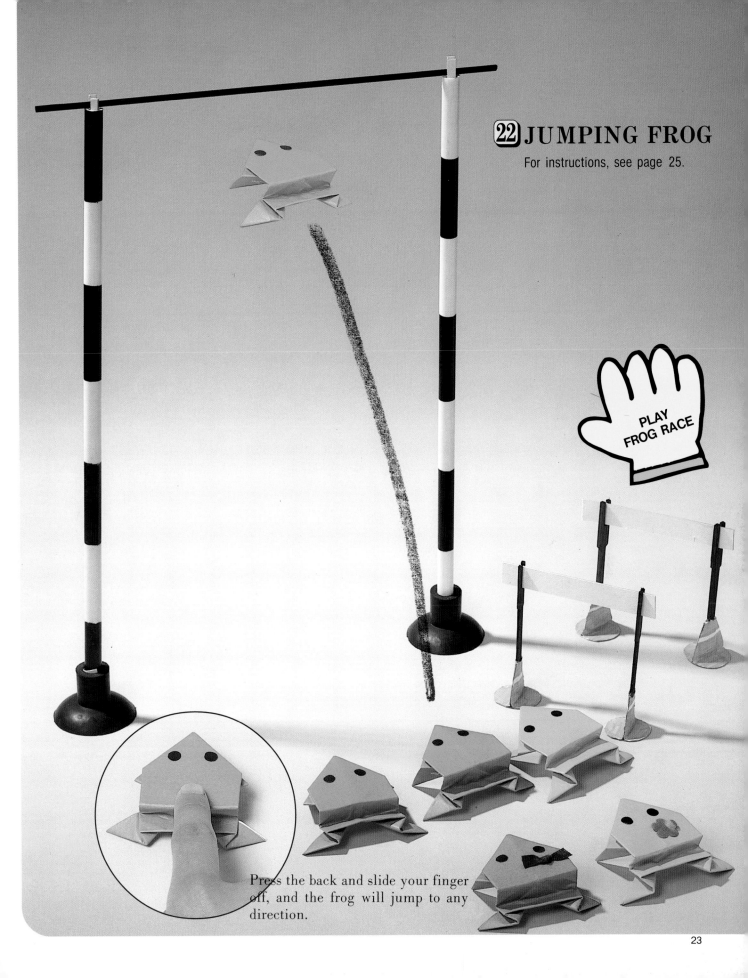

22 JUMPING FROG

For instructions, see page 25.

PLAY FROG RACE

Press the back and slide your finger off, and the frog will jump to any direction.

Use 6"×6" paper

SOMERSAULTING HORSE

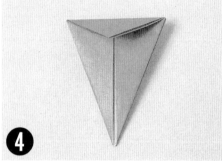

1 Begin with white side up. Fold in half and unfold; repeat to make valley folds crosswise. Unfold and turn over. Fold and unfold twice diagonally.

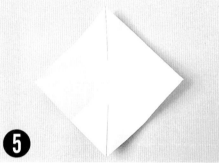

2 Press down using the creases.

3 Fold up lower edges to meet at the center.

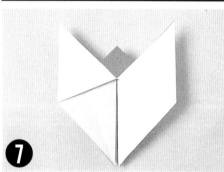

4 Turn over and repeat. Fold down the upper triangle.

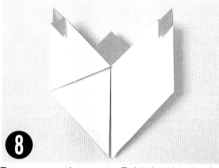

5 Unfold and make slits.

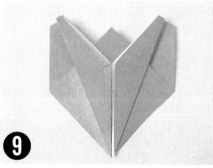

6 Fold again into the former shape.

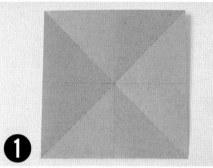

7 Fold up flaps diagonally from the side corners.

8 Turn over and repeat. Fold the tips back.

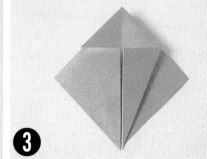

9 Fold in sides to align at the center.

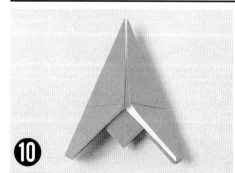

10 Turn over and repeat. Rotate to make ½ turn.

11 Make head and tail by folding the tips inside.

12 Fold the tip of head inside for completed horse.

1 Fold in half to make a rectangle.

2 Fold again in half to make a square.

3 Unfold once. On upper square, make diagonal valley folds.

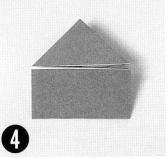

4 Unfold and valley fold along the middle. Push in sides using the creases.

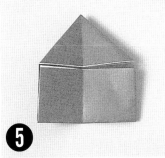

5 Fold vertically in half to make a crease.

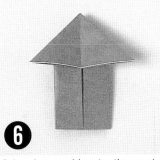

6 Bring lower sides to the center and fold under the top triangle.

7 Fold up bottom edges of triangle diagonally.

8 Fold up the bottom in half.

9 Fold back the corners into triangles.

10 Unfold and pull the inner corner to the side. Press down to fold.

11 Repeat on the other side.

12 Fold down the sides to make legs

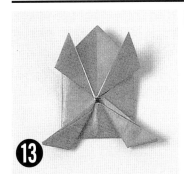

13 Fold back diagonally from the top.

14 Fold up bottom along the middle crease.

15 Fold it back in half.

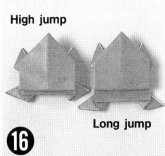

High jump

Long jump

16 Turn over for completed frog. Jumping style depends on the width of the final fold.

23 SNAIL

For instructions, see page 28.

24 TADPOLE

For instructions, see page 29.

25 FROG

For instructions, see page 29.

Use 6"×6" paper

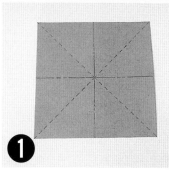

❶ Begin with white side up. Make valley folds crosswise. Unfold and turn over. Fold and unfold twice diagonally.

❷ Press down using the creases.

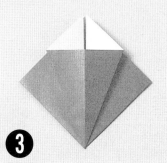

❸ Lift one corner upright, insert your finger into opening and press down to fold.

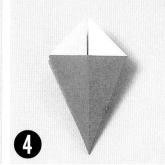

❹ Repeat on all flaps.

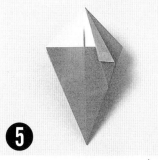

❺ Fold in right upper edge by ⅓.

❻ Fold again to align with the center.

❼ Fold in left upper edge in half, to align with the center.

❽ Turn over and repeat.

❾ Right side is folded twice, left side once.

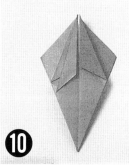

❿ Flip one over. Fold the right side in half, the left side in three.

⓫ Turn over and repeat.

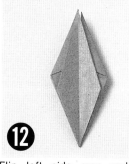

⓬ Flip left side over and press down. Turn over and repeat.

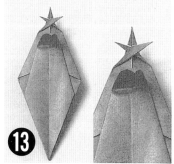

⓭ Fold in points overlapping each other.

⓮ Fold down the bottom tip and fold the uppermost tip under so as to cover it. Glue to secure.

⓯ Fold up the bottom half.

⓰ Unfold and pull out pleats to both sides to form plump shell.

FROG

 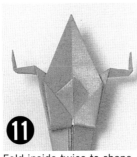 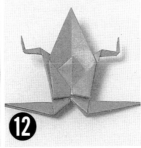  

 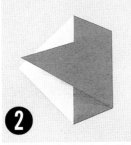 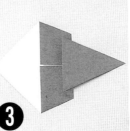 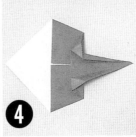 

Use 6"×6" paper

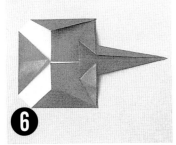 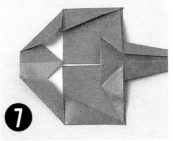  

25 on page 27

5 For steps ① - ④, refer to SNAIL (opposite page). Rotate upside down. Fold lower edges to align with the center.

6 Unfold. Lift the center and press down to fold.

7 Repeat on all four sides.

8 Fold sides again to the center to make narrow legs.

9 Flip and repeat to make four legs.

10 Fold up upper legs making inside fold.

11 Fold inside twice to shape fore legs.

12 Fold up remaining legs horizontally making inside fold.

13 Fold inside twice to shape hind legs.

14 Pull sides to form plump body for completed frog.

TADPOLE

Use 2"×2" paper

24 on page 26

1 Begin with white side up. Fold diagonally in half and unfold. Bring sides to meet at the center.

2 Fold lengthwise in half.

3 Fold back the tip.

4 Fold in one side to make narrow tail. Press down the triangle just formed.

5 Fold in the other side and press down the triangle formed.

6 Fold in top, bottom, and side corners.

7 Fold in remaining white sections.

8 Turn over and mountain fold any corner to smooth out the edges.

9 Mountain fold the tail and body for plump tadpole.

29

26 SQUID

For instructions, see page 32.

27 OCTOPUS

For instructions, see page 32.

Attach a paper clip to the mouth of the fish. Scatter several fish, hang a magnet from a stick and pretend you are fishing.

GO FISHING!

28 FISH

For instructions, see page 33.

29 FLYING FISH

For instructions, see page 33.
This is a variation of FISH(above).

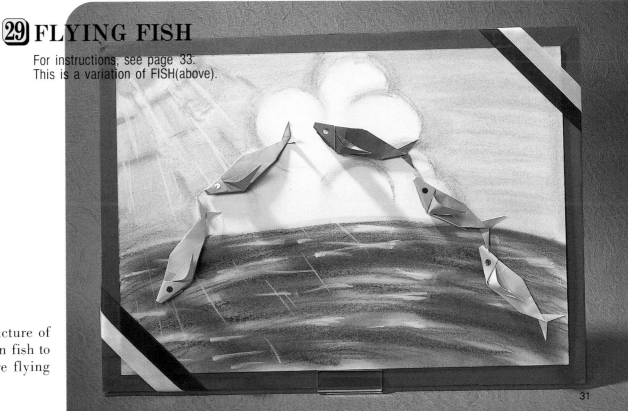

Draw or paint a picture of the sea and glue on fish to show as if they are flying above the waters.

26 on page 30
SQUID
Use 6"×6" paper

27 on page 30
OCTOPUS
Use 6"×6" paper

1 Begin with white side up. Fold in half and unfold; repeat to make valley folds crosswise. Turn over. Fold and unfold twice diagonally.

2 Press down using the creases.

3 Fold in lower edges to meet at the center.

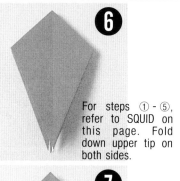

6 For steps ① - ⑤, refer to SQUID on this page. Fold down upper tip on both sides.

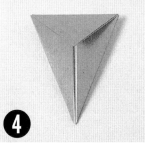

4 Turn over and repeat. Fold down the top corner.

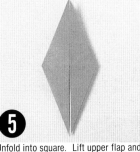

5 Unfold into square. Lift upper flap and fold in sides using the creases just formed to make a diamond. Turn over and repeat.

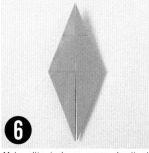

6 Make slits (only on upper sheet) at 1⅜" from the top inserting scissors from opening.

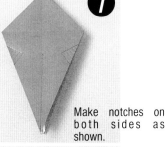

7 Make notches on both sides as shown.

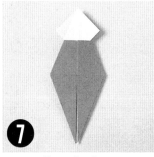

7 Open the top.

8 Turn over and fold down the upper point.

9 Fold down the center corner and then fold up to make "Z" fold.

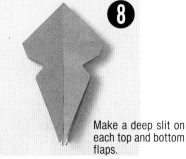

8 Make a deep slit on each top and bottom flaps.

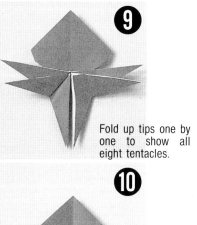

9 Fold up tips one by one to show all eight tentacles.

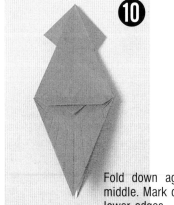

10 Fold down again along the middle. Mark deep slits along lower edges.

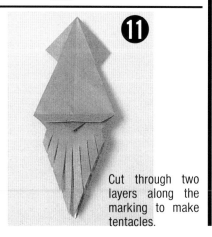

11 Cut through two layers along the marking to make tentacles.

10 Turn over for completed octopus.

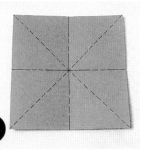

① Begin with white side up. Fold in half and unfold; repeat to make valley folds crosswise. Turn over. Fold and unfold twice diagonally.

② Press down using the creases. Fold in lower edges to meet at the center.

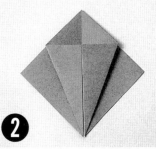

③ Turn over and repeat. Unfold into square. Lift upper flap and fold in sides using the creases just formed to make a diamond. Turn over and repeat.

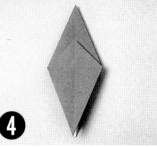

④ Fold down one flap.

⑤ Fold in half lengthwise. Rotate so the longest edge faces you, bulky tip facing the left.

⑥ Fold back one flap at $1\frac{3}{4}$" from the tip. Turn over and repeat.

⑦ Fold bottom corner diagonally. Turn over and repeat.

⑧ Unfold the triangle and fold under.

⑨ Using middle flap, wrap the end, working upwards and then downwards.

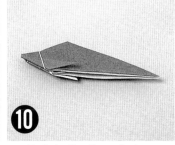

⑩ Tuck in the tip and glue.

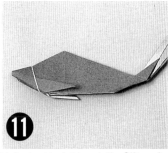

⑪ Make inside fold on tail. Slit end.

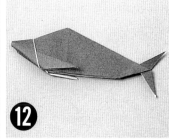

⑫ Fold down one tail for completed fish.

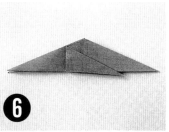

⑥ For steps ①-⑤, refer to FISH (above). Fold back one flap at $2\frac{1}{4}$" from the tip.

⑦ Fold bottom corner, diagonally under. Fold top corners inside.

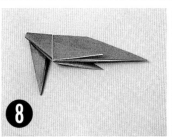

⑧ Using the middle flap, wrap the end, working upwards and downwards. Tuck in the end.

⑨ Make tail as for FISH.

30 DOVE

For instructions, see page 36.

31 FLAPPING BIRD

For instructions, see page 36.

34

32 SWALLOW

For instructions, see page 36.

33 BABY SWALLOW

For instructions, see page 37.

34 LACY DOVE

For instructions, see page 36.

To. MAMA

Steps ① - ④ are common to all models.

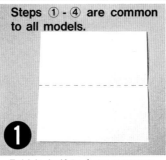

① Fold in half to form a crease.

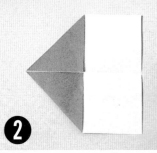

② Fold two corners to align at the center.

③ Fold down in half.

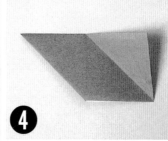

④ Form a crease by folding upper right corner to match the bottom center and unfold.

SWALLOW/FLAPPING BIRD

⑤ Fold in the side to align the crease.

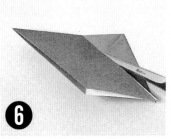

⑥ Male a slit along the crease through two layers.

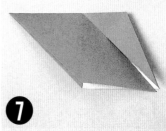

⑦ Fold under the triangle formed in step ⑤.

⑧ Fold up the center flap to form wing. Turn over and repeat.

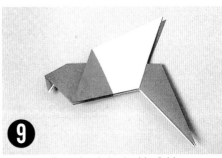

⑨ Form beak by inside fold.

DOVE

⑤ After step ④, mark as shown and trim away.

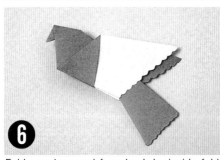

⑥ Fold up wings and form beak by inside fold.

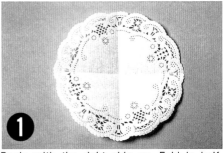

① Begin with the right side up. Fold in half twice and unfold.

② Fold in two sides so as to connect the creases.

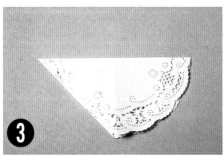

③ Fold down in half.

BABY SWALLOW

Use 4"×4" paper

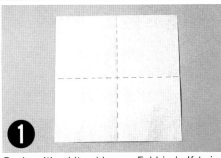

1 Begin with white side up. Fold in half twice and unfold.

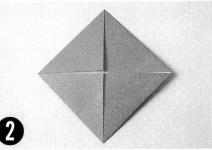

2 Bring all corners to meet at the center (cushion fold).

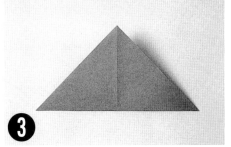

3 Fold up in half.

4 Fold down ⅖ of the height.

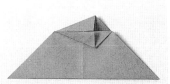

5 Unfold and fold two edges to meet at the center.

6 Unfold and work on remaining edges the same.

7 Unfold and let stand to form beak.

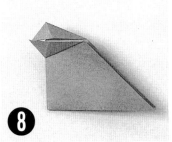

8 Fold in half.

9 Fold back one flap diagonally from the end of beak.

10 Fold back diagonally from the bottom corner. Turn over and repeat.

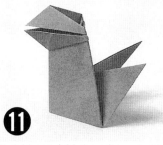

11 Unfold and fold the other way so as to tuck in the tail.

LACY DOVE

4 Make diagonal crease by folding down the right edge.

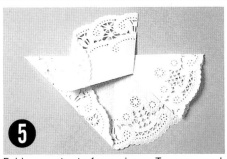

5 Fold up center to form wings. Turn over and repeat.

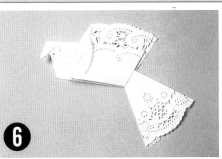

6 Form beak by folding the tip under.

35 MACAW

For instructions, see page 41.

36 BABY BIRD

For instructions, see page 40.

37 CANARY

For instructions, see page 40.

38 WAGTAIL

For instructions, see page 41.

Use 6"×6" paper

BABY BIRD

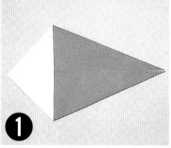

①

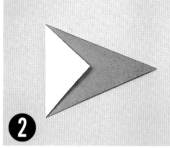

②

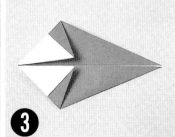

③

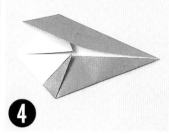

④

Fold in half diagonally. Unfold and bring sides to meet at the center.

Turn over and fold in the triangle.

Turn over again and fold in corners to the center.

Open the center and pull out flaps.

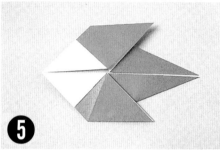

⑤

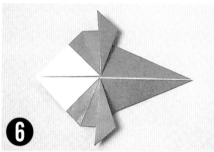

⑥

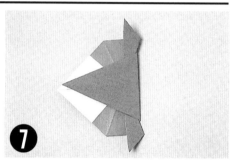

⑦

Flip them towards the narrower tip.

Fold back ⅓ from the edge to form legs.

Fold in half.

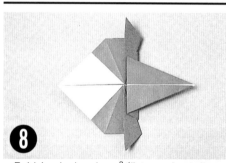

⑧

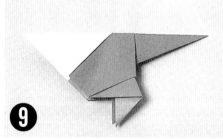

⑨

⑩

Fold back, leaving ⅜" to make tail.

Mountain fold along the center.

Form beak by inside fold. Pull out tail for completed baby bird.

Use 6"×6" paper

CANARY

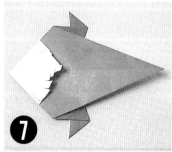

⑦

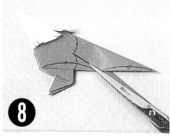

⑧

⑨

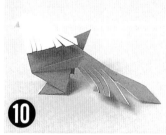

⑩

For steps ① – ⑥, refer to BABY BIRD (above). Turn over and make slits at ⅛" intervals.

Mountain fold in half. Make a slit from the center of bottom to the middle of height.

Form beak by inside fold. Fold up wings on both sides.

Make deep slits on tail for completed canary.

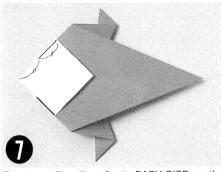

7 For steps ① – ⑥, refer to BABY BIRD on the opposite page. Turn over and make slits on the upper flap.

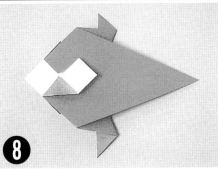

8 Fold in corners to meet at the center.

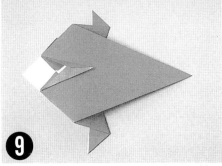

9 Form tapered crest by folding sides overlapping each other. Glue to secure.

10 Mountain fold in half. Form beak by folding the white section inside. Mountain fold the crest so as to stand.

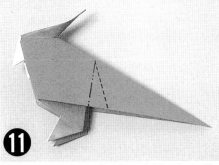

11 Make mountain and valley folds along the folding dots.

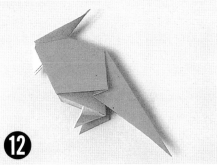

12 Push in the valley fold to form wing. Turn over and repeat for completed macaw.

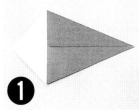

1 Fold in half diagonally. Unfold and bring sides to meet at the center.

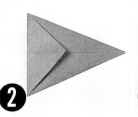

2 Fold in the triangle.

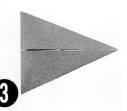

3 Tuck in the triangle.

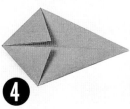

4 Fold corners to meet at the center.

5 Open the center and pull out flaps.

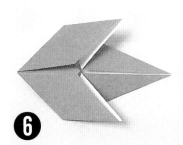

6 Flip them towards the narrower tip.

7 Fold back ⅓ from the edge to form legs.

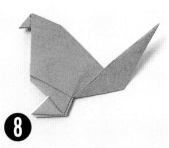

8 Make a crease by folding up the tail.

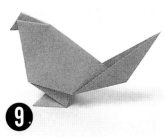

9 Make a cover fold on tail for completed wagtail.

39 SWAN

For instructions, see page 44.

40 BABY SWAN

For instructions, see page 44.

41 WATER BIRD

For instructions, see page 45.

42 DUCKLING

For instructions, see page 44.

1 Fold in half diagonally. Unfold and bring sides to meet at the center.

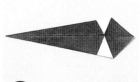

2 Turn over and fold in sides to align with the center.

3 Fold in half.

4 Mountain fold in half lengthwise.

5 Lift the tip.

Variation

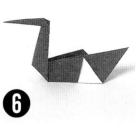

6 Make cover fold to form head.

7 Make mountain and valley folds on the tip to form beak. Flatten the beak.

6 After step ⑤, fold neck by inside fold so as to face backwards.

7 Form head by making cover fold.

8 Mountain fold the tip, then valley fold to form beak.

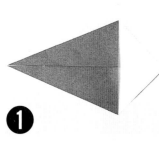

1 Fold in half diagonally. Unfold and bring sides to meet at the center.

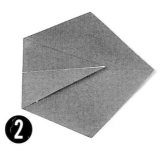

2 Turn over. Fold back pointed end, leaving a little space from the other end.

3 Mountain fold in half.

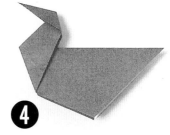

4 Pull up the flap and press down the base. Cover fold the tip to form head.

5 Mountain fold the tip, then valley fold to form beak.

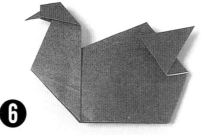

6 Make another alternate fold on the other end to form tail.

7 Fold the tail under for completion.

1 Use either round or square cut paper. Fold in half.

2 Fold in half again.

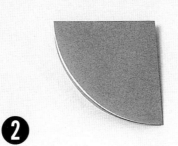

3 Open the upper flap towards right and press down to fold.

4 Turn over and repeat to match.

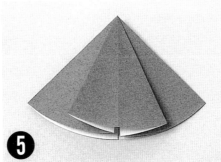

5 Now open the left-hand fold and press down. Repeat on the remaining folds.

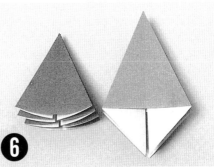

6 Folded round paper and square paper.

7 Fold in half so the flaps face you.

8 Make cover fold in the middle to form neck.

9 Cover fold again to form head.

10 Fold up the top flaps diagonally.

11 Fold up the layers gradating to form wings.

12 Fold the bottom flaps under.

44 FLAMINGO

For instructions, see page 49.

45 CRANE

For instructions,
see page 48.

46 CRANE PENDANT

For instructions, see page 48.

❶

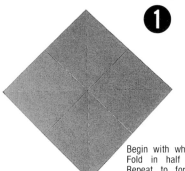

Begin with white side up. Fold in half and unfold. Repeat to form crisscross valley fold. Turn over. Fold and unfold twice diagonally.

❷

Press down using the creases.

❸

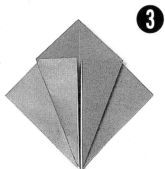

Fold in lower edges to meet at the center.

❹

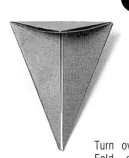

Turn over and repeat. Fold down the top corner.

❺

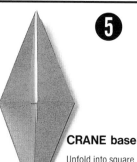

CRANE base

Unfold into square. Lift upper flap and fold in sides using the creases just formed to make a diamond. Turn over and repeat.

❻

Fold in lower sides to align with the center.

❼

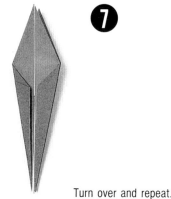

Turn over and repeat.

❽

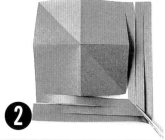

Bring up the points and press down the bases. Make inside fold on one point.

❾

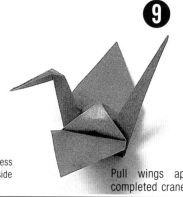

Pull wings apart for completed crane.

❶

Begin with colored side up. Fold in half diagonally and make alternate slits as shown.

❷

Cut inner two bands at the corner to make loop. Fold the square in half twice.

❸

Start folding CRANE referring steps ① – ⑥ (above).

❹

Completed crane pendant.

5

Make a CRANE base referring steps ① - ⑤ on opposite page.

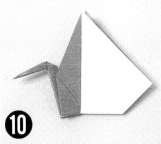

6

Unfold one side and fold inside out upwards along the creases.

7

Bring the corner to match the top and fold inside.

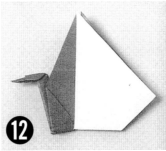

8

Fold in lower side to align with the center.

9

Turn over and repeat.

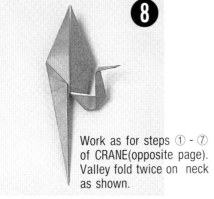

10

Bring up the tip and fold inside. Form head by inside fold.

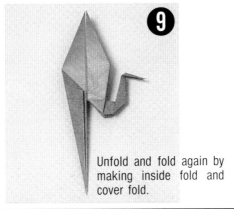

11

Flatten the head and make "Z" fold to form beak.

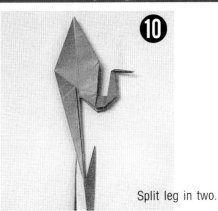

12

Press the head between your thumb and finger to fold in half.

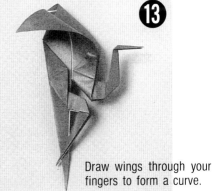

13

Fold down wings for completed peacock.

8

Work as for steps ① - ⑦ of CRANE(opposite page). Valley fold twice on neck as shown.

9

Unfold and fold again by making inside fold and cover fold.

10

Split leg in two.

11

Fold one leg as shown.

12

Unfold and fold again by making inside fold.

13

Draw wings through your fingers to form a curve.

FINE FLOWERS

Flowers would be the best element with which children can experience the seasons. Share time and fun by creating flowers of the season. Don't just let children fold them and throw them away. Keep them and decorate your home with imaginative displays.

47 3D TULIP

For instructions, see page 52.

48 FLAT TULIP

For instructions, see page 53.

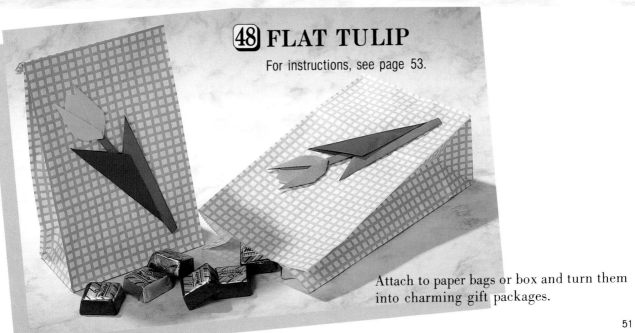

Attach to paper bags or box and turn them into charming gift packages.

❶ Fold in half. Unfold and repeat to make creases.

❷ Bring all four corners to the center.

❸ Fold in half.

❹ Fold in half again.

❺ Lift the upper flap and press down to fold to make square. Turn over and repeat.

❻ Rotate to make ½ turn. Fold in side corners at a slant.

❼ Turn over and repeat.

❽ Bring sides and glue, aligning the edges.

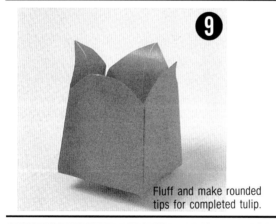

❾ Fluff and make rounded tips for completed tulip.

❶ Fold in half diagonally to make a crease.

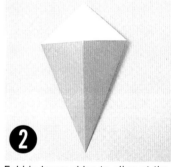

❷ Fold in lower sides to align at the center.

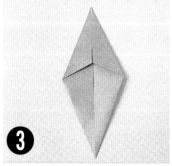

❸ Fold in upper sides.

❹ Fold lengthwise in half. Completion of narrow leaf.

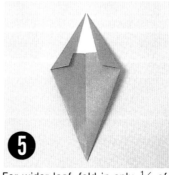

❺ For wider leaf, fold in only ⅓ of the upper sides.

❻ Fold lengthwise in half for completion of wide leaf. Combine leaves of both widths.

FLAT TULIP

Use 3"×3" paper

    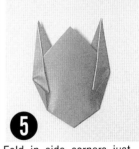

1 Fold in half to make a triangle.

2 Fold up diagonally from a bottom point beyond the center.

3 Fold up the other side in the same manner.

4 Turn over and fold in side corners.

5 Fold in side corners just formed.

10

6 Turn over for completed tulip.

7 Make stem. Cut 6" square paper into quarters lengthwise. Each strip makes one stem.

8 Fold lengthwise in half.

9 Fold in half again and glue to secure.

Completed tulip. Combine two wider leaves.

EASY VEINED LEAF

Use 6"diam paper

  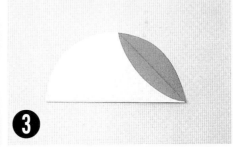

1 If round origami is not in hand, trim square paper.

2 Fold in half.

3 Fold down diagonally along the line connecting the side and top points.

4 Fold up bottom edge diagonally.

5 Make pleated folds to form veins.

6 Unfold for completed leaf. Make leaves for HYDRANGEA in the same manner.

49 EASY FLOWER

For flower, see page 56.
For leaf, see page 53.

50 DANDELION

For instructions, see page 56.

Wrap stems with floral tape and attach a safety pin to make a broach.

51 CARNATION

For instructions, see page 57.

A side view. Sepals are added for more appeal.

1 Use round paper. If unavailable, trim square origami.

2 Begin with colored side up. Fold up in half.

3 Fold in half again.

4 Open the upper flap towards right and press down to fold. Turn over and repeat to match.

5 Open a fold and press down. Repeat on the remaining three folds.

6 Open the six folds and repeat step ⑤.

7 Now 16 flaps are folded.

8 Fold in half.

9

10

1 Make flowers referring EASY FLOWER (above) in two different sizes. Make slits on $1\frac{1}{8}" \times 2\frac{1}{4}"$ paper for center.

2 Roll up the slitted rectangle. Insert into smaller flower.

3 Insert this into larger flower.

4 Bind the base of flower with wire.

5 Join a bamboo skewer or thick wire and secure with wire.

6 Wrap the stem with floral tape for completed dandelion.

1 Use three sheets (of *washi* paper if preferred). Trim edges of paper with pinking shears.

2 Layer three sheets and make accordion pleats at $\frac{1}{4}$" intervals. Be sure to make pleats on trimmed edges.

3 Bind the center with wire.

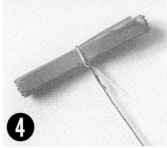

4 Attach thick wire to the center to make stem.

5 Spread out the pleats.

6 Lift each petal to stand so it resembles a carnation petal.

7 Tear facial tissue paper into $\frac{1}{2}$" width and wrap the base. Glue the end to secure.

8 Cover the base with sepal (see below) for completed carnation.

1 Begin with CRANE base (see page 48, steps ① - ⑤).

2 Fold down upper half and rotate to make $\frac{1}{2}$ turn.

3 Fold upper sides to align with the center.

4 Unfold one fold and press down the bottom triangle.

5 Do the same on the other side. Turn over and repeat.

6 Flip over one flap and fold upper sides to meet at the center.

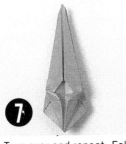

7 Turn over and repeat. Fold lower sides to meet at the center. Flip and repeat on

8 Pull the tips apart.

9 Fold inner corners to enlarge the hole.

10 Completed sepal viewed from the reverse side.

52 SUNFLOWER

For instructions, see page 60.

53 BOAT

For instructions,
see page 60.

54 LILY

For instructions,
see page 61.

① Begin with colored side up. Fold in half to make a crease.

② Fold edges to align with the center.

③ Fold in corners to match the center.

④ Fold top and bottom corners, matching the center.

⑤ Fold top and bottom corners to meet at the center.

⑥ Open one side from the center and fold inside out.

⑦ Repeat on the other side for completed boat. For sunflower petals, make 16 and press down flat.

⑧ On a small round base, glue 4 petals.

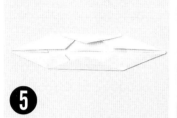

⑨ Glue 4 more petals. This makes the bottom layer.

⑩ Glue 8 petals onto the first layer so the bottom petals peek between the top petals.

Flower center

① Use 6"×6" paper. Begin with colored side up. Fold in half.

② Fold in half again.

③ Fold in half again. If the layers are too thick to fold, fold each half separately.

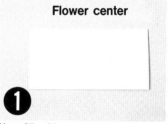

④ Fold in half again. Now the paper is divided into 16.

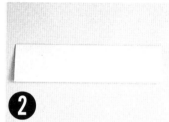

⑤ Unfold. Mountain fold and valley fold alternately.

⑥ Unfold and make vertical creases in the same manner. Unfold.

⑦ Bring the first vertical mountain-fold to half way to the next valley fold. Then fold down the top horizontal crease in the same manner.

⑧ Continue folding shallow pleats until all creases are folded.

⑨ Turn over and fold in all edges.

⑩ Glue onto the petals for completed sunflower.

LILY

1 Begin with colored side up. Fold in half and fold back one corner to match the fold.

2 Cut along the edge of the colored paper to make a right-angle triangle.

3 Fold two long sides in half.

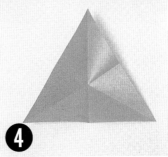

4 Now three creases intersect at the center.

5 Make deep slits on all sides.

6 Turn over and make center crease on each.

7 Unfold and fold in half.

8 Unfold and bring three points together. The center becomes the peak.

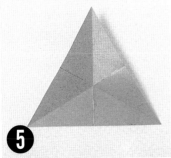

9 Fold side corners to match at the center.

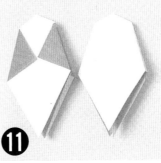

10 Flip and repeat until all corners are folded.

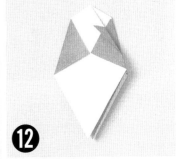

11 Make two. On the second model, tuck in the corners and glue.

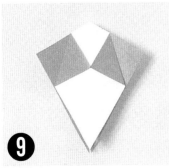

12 For the first model, fold a shoulder point to align with the center.

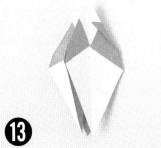

13 Flip and repeat on all shoulder points.

14 Curl the petal ends.

15 Finish the second model in the same manner.

16 Insert the first model into the second one.

55 MORNING GLORY

For instructions, see page 64.

Glue onto fan for a cool, 3D effect. Leaves and vines can be drawn directly on the surface.

56 HYDRANGEA

For instructions, see page 64.

Just scatter on a glass plate to create a mood.

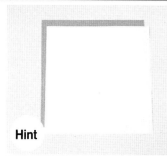

Hint

If shaded origami is unavailable, lay white origami on colored one, and trim the white into a diamond shape when finished.

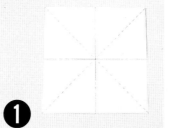

1 Begin with colored side up. Fold in half. Unfold and repeat. Turn over and fold in half diagonally. Unfold and repeat.

2 Press down using the creases.

3 Fold up lower edges to meet at the center. Turn over and repeat.

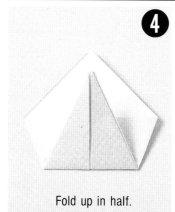

4 Fold up in half.

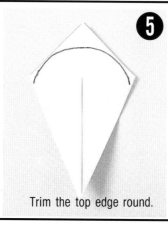

5 Trim the top edge round.

6 Open the top along the middle crease for completed flower.

56 on page 63

HYDRANGEA

Use 1"×1" paper

3 For steps ① and ②, refer to MORNING GLORY (above). Rotate to make ½ turn. Fold up bottom corner.

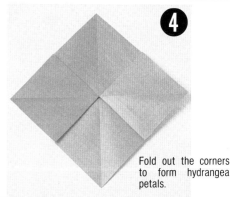

4 Fold out the corners to form hydrangea petals.

1 Begin with white side up. Fold in half. Unfold and fold in half again.

2 Bring edges to align with the middle crease.

3 Turn over and fold sides to meet at the center.

4 Fold down in half.

5 Make handles with spare paper and glue on.

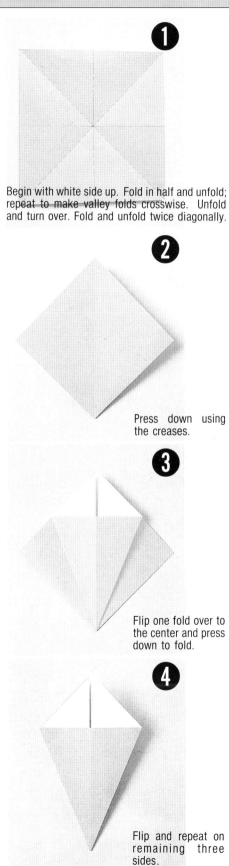

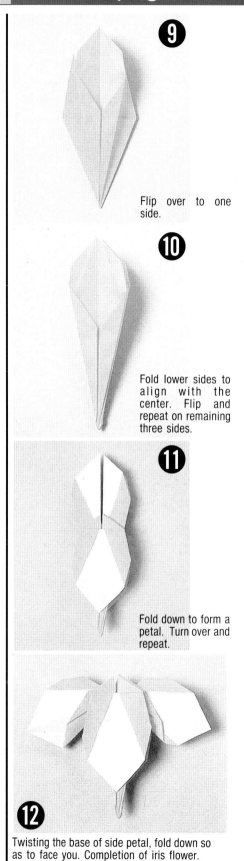

1

Begin with white side up. Fold in half and unfold; repeat to make valley folds crosswise. Unfold and turn over. Fold and unfold twice diagonally.

2

Press down using the creases.

3

Flip one fold over to the center and press down to fold.

4

Flip and repeat on remaining three sides.

5

Fold upper sides to meet at the center.

6

Unfold and pull out the center. Press down to make a diamond.

7

Open the top to show some of white side. Fold sides, overlapping at the bottom.

8

Fold up the center flap. Repeat on remaining three sides.

9

Flip over to one side.

10

Fold lower sides to align with the center. Flip and repeat on remaining three sides.

11

Fold down to form a petal. Turn over and repeat.

12

Twisting the base of side petal, fold down so as to face you. Completion of iris flower.

57 IRIS

For instructions, see page 65.

58 LOTUS

For instructions,
see page 68.

Rippled leaves are made of
crepe paper.

Use 6"×6" paper

LOTUS

1 Fold in half. Unfold and repeat to make creases.

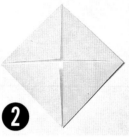

2 Bring all four corners to the center(cushion fold).

3 Bring all four corners again to the center.

4 Repeat to make an even smaller square.

5 Turn over and fold in corners. Press tightly to fold.

6 Raise a corner on the reverse side so as to stand.

7 Raise remaining corners as well.

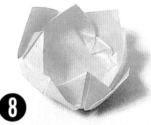

8 Raise the middle layer of corners on the reverse side so as to stand.

9 Repeat with the final layer of corners to form completed lotus.

Use 8"×8" paper

TABLE

1 Begin with white side up. Make valley folds diagonally. Unfold and make valley folds horizontally and vertically into ¼.

2 Bring up all four corners folding each in half.

3 Fold in edges.

4 Inserting your finger into folded corner and press down to fold into a square.

5 Fold all corners.

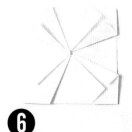

6 Fold sides of each square to align with the center.

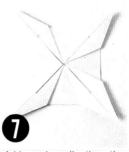

7 Unfold and pull the tip outwards. Press down to make a diamond. Repeat to make four diamonds.

8 Fold in tips to match the crease.

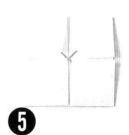

9 Fold in again to make legs.

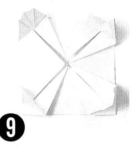

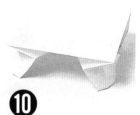

10 Turn over to stand for completed table.

FLYING PLANE:A

Use rectangular paper such as B4 notebook leaf

(header) 59 on page 70

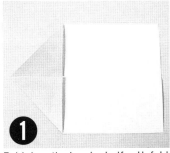

1 Fold lengthwise in half. Unfold and fold in corners.

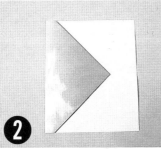

2 Fold in the point at $\frac{3}{4}$" beyond the bottom of triangle.

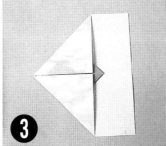

3 Fold in the corners again to meet at the center. Note the peeking corner.

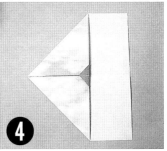

4 Fold back the small triangle.

5 Mountain fold in half. Fold up bottom edge diagonally under the triangle, to form a crease.

6 Refold along this crease, pushing the bottom edge inside. Bring down the fold to align with the bottom.

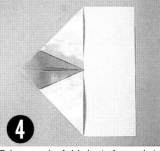

7 Turn over and repeat for completed plane.

FLYING PLANE:C

Use rectangular paper such as B4 notebook leaf

61 on page 70

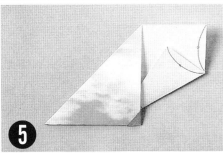

1 Begin with white side up. Make diagonal valley folds aligning edges. Mountain fold vertically through the cross just formed.

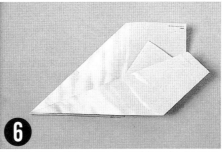

2 Fold along the creases, pushing in top and bottom edges.

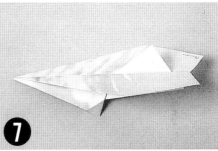

3 Fold the points towards the left to match the peak.

4 Bring each fold just formed to meet at the center.

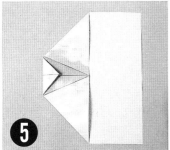

5 Fold in the peak so as to form a triangle. Make a slit all through the layers.

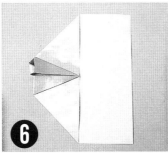

6 Lift left-hand point and tuck into pockets just made.

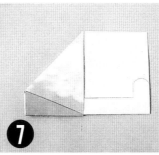

7 Mountain fold in half. Mark as above and cut along the line.

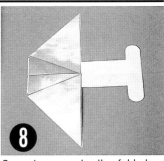

8 Spread open and valley fold along the center.

MAKE YOUR OWN TOYS

Enjoy origami twice. Have fun folding paper, and play with the model you just made! As your skill develops, you can add infinite ideas for models and find new way to play.

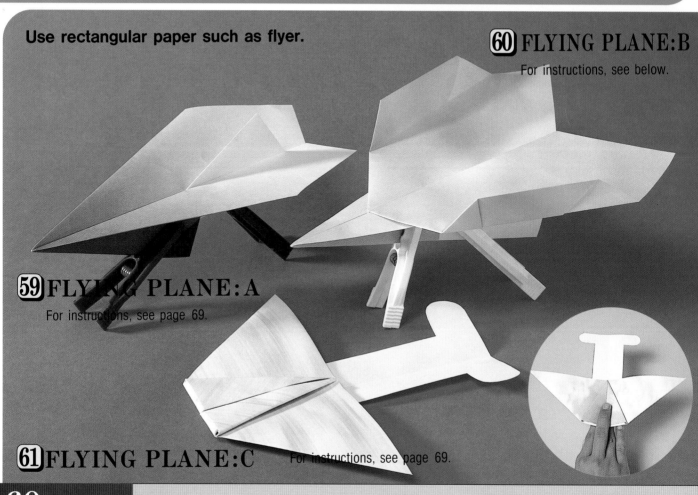

Use rectangular paper such as flyer.

60 FLYING PLANE:B
For instructions, see below.

59 FLYING PLANE:A
For instructions, see page 69.

61 FLYING PLANE:C   For instructions, see page 69.

---

60   Use B4 size paper   FLYING PLANE:B

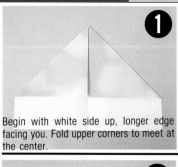

1 Begin with white side up, longer edge facing you. Fold upper corners to meet at the center.

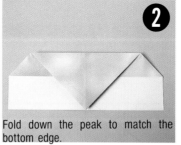

2 Fold down the peak to match the bottom edge.

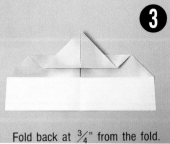

3 Fold back at $\frac{3}{4}$" from the fold.

4 Mountain fold in half and place the fold towards you.

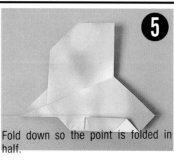

5 Fold down so the point is folded in half.

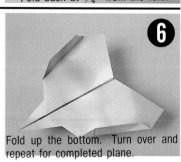

6 Fold up the bottom. Turn over and repeat for completed plane.

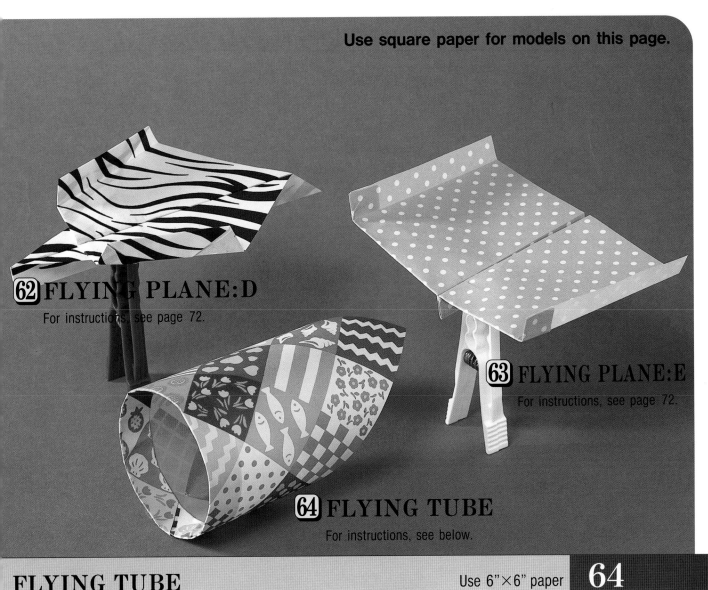

62 FLYING PLANE:D

For instructions, see page 72.

63 FLYING PLANE:E

For instructions, see page 72.

64 FLYING TUBE

For instructions, see below.

FLYING TUBE

Use 6"×6" paper **64**

❶

Fold in half to make a triangle.

❷

Unfold and fold up a corner matching with the crease.

❸

Fold the flap in half so the bottom fold aligns with the crease.

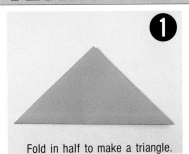

❹

Fold the flap in half, and fold up again so the middle crease becomes the bottom.

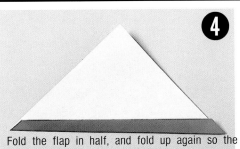

❺

Bring up side points and insert one end into another for completed flying tube.

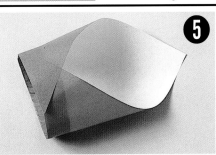

❶ Fold in half to make a triangle. Unfold and fold two sides to align at the center.

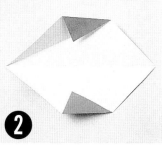

❷ Unfold. Fold in corners, aligning one edge with the crease.

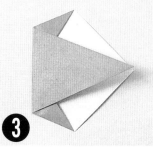

❸ Hold in the sides again along the creases. Fold in half.

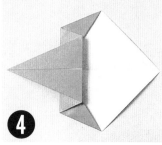

❹ Fold back so the new fold matches the bottom folds.

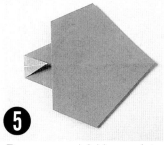

❺ Turn over and fold up point.

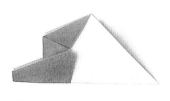

❻ Fold up in half.

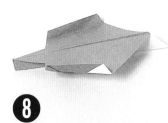

❼ Fold down upper wing so the fold lies horizontally from top of head. Fold up bottom.

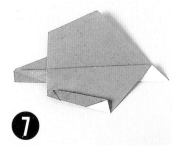

❽ Turn over and repeat for completed plane.

❶

Begin with white side up. Fold up in half.

❷ Unfold and fold up the bottom edge to align with the middle crease.

❸ Fold the flap in three.

❹ Unfold. Fold under along the creases.

❺ Mountain fold in half.

❻

Fold down top edge so the fold is made $\frac{3}{8}$" above the middle. Fold up bottom edge.

❼ Turn over and repeat for completed plane.

1 Fold in half. Make center crease.

2 Bring sides to the center.

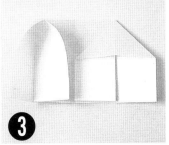

3 Unfold and open up a flap. Press down to fold a triangle on top.

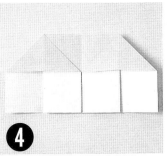

4 Repeat on the other side.

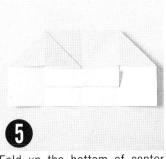

5 Fold up the bottom of center flap in half.

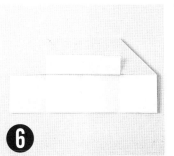

6 Fold up again.

7 Fold in sides.

8 Raise the center fold to make keyboard. Raise the sides to stand the completed piano.

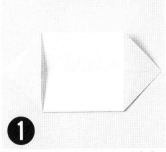

1 Make center crease and bring all four corners to the center.

2 Turn over and fold up triangles to meet at the center.

3 Turn over and fold up all corners to meet at the center.

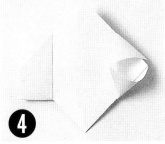

4 Turn over again. Pull the small pockets outwards and press down to fold.

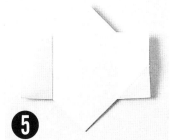

5 Small rectangles are made on both sides.

6 Turn over. Fold in points to meet at the center.

7 Fold lengthwise in half.

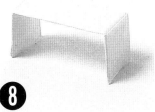

8 Fold up side squares and stand for completed stool.

65 PIANO   For instructions, see page 73.

66 PIANO STOOL

For instructions, see page 73.

67 TABLE

For instructions, see page 68.

68 CHAIR

For instructions,
see page 84.

A variation in color and texture. Use thicker paper for stability.

Use 6"×6" paper

1 Begin with white side up. Fold into half to make a triangle. Fold upper edge down to align with the bottom.

2 Unfold. Bring one point up to meet the end of crease.

3 Fold the other point up symmetrically.

4 Fold down one flap.

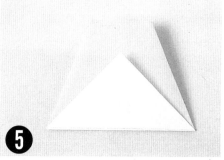

5 Turn over and repeat. Rotate to make ½ turn.

6 Open up the bottom and stand. Squash the top.

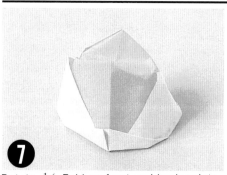

7 Rotate ¼. Fold up front and back points.

8 Pull the triangular flaps towards both sides to form brim. The brim can be rounded by cutting.

Variation

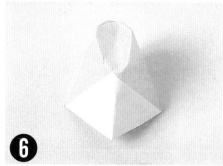

6 Fold as for steps ① - ⑤. Fold down one upper side of the triangle to align with the bottom.

7 Turn over and repeat.

8 Squash the top.

9 Trim one flap to form a round brim.

❶ Fold in half to make a triangle.

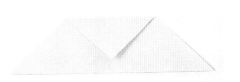

❷ Fold down peak to meet the center of bottom edge.

❸ Unfold. Fold sides to align with the horizontal crease.

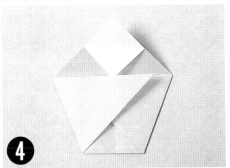

❹ Fold down one flap into half.

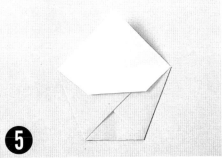

❺ Fold down again along the crease.

❻ Turn over. Rotate to make ½ turn and fold up the flap.

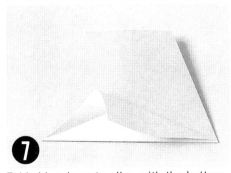

❼ Fold sides down to align with the bottom. Unfold.

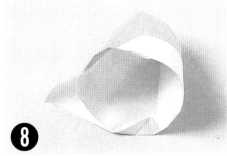

❽ Open up and squash the top. Fold corners inside.

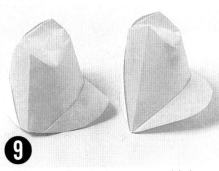

❾ Trim one flap to form a round brim.

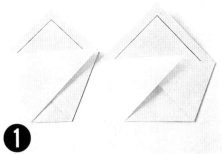

❶ Fold referring steps ① - ③ of either HAT or CAP. Mark as shown.

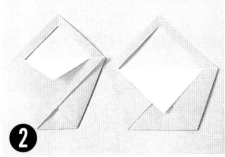

❷ Fold down inner triangles and glue to secure. Push up the bottom for fullness.

PARASOL

71 JAPANESE UMBRELLA

For instructions,
see page 80.

69 PARASOL

For instructions,
see page 80.

70 UMBRELLA

For instructions,
see page 81.

BAG & CAP

72 CAP

For instructions,
see page 77.

73 HAT

For instructions,
see page 76.

75 BAG:B

For instructions,
see page 64.

74 BAG:A

For instructions, see page 77.

PARASOL

1 Refer to steps ① - ⑤ on opposite page. Trim into scalloped edges.

2 Make two. On one model, make slits near the peak.

3 Turn slitted model, inside out except the center. Refold all outer creases; mountain fold into valley fold, valley fold into mountain fold.

4 Spread out the other model and make a hole in the center.

5 Make a hole on the slitted one and glue onto the outer shade.

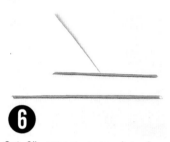

6 Cut 6" square paper into long quarters. Roll one strip tightly to form a handle.

7 Insert the handle through the holes and glue onto the peak.

8 Insert wire through the handle. Make a curve on one end.

9 Completed parasol. Use paper doily for a fancier parasol.

JAPANESE UMBRELLA

1 Refer to steps ① - ⑤ on opposite page. Double the creases: Open one pocket and push the sides in. Press down the center to form layers of diamond.

2 Repeat on remainings three sides. Make two in different colors.

3 Trim tops away. Make the inner shade about $\frac{1}{8}$" shorter.

4 Make slits (see step ② above) on inner shade.

5 Turn the slitted shade inside out except the center. Refold all outer creases: mountain fold into valley fold, valley fold into mountain fold.

6 Spread out the outer shade and pierce a hole in the center.

7 Stick two shades together with glue. Pierce the inner shade and insert a handle(see steps ⑥ - ⑧ above).

UMBRELLA

1

Begin with white side up. Make valley folds crosswise. Turn over. Fold and unfold twice diagonally.

2

Press down using the creases.

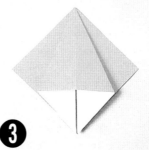

3

Lift one corner upright, insert your finger into opening and press down to fold.

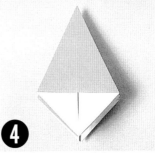

4

Repeat on all flaps.

5

Flip one side over. Turn over and repeat.

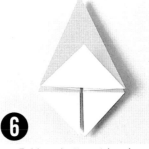

6

Fold up bottom triangle.

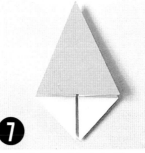

7

Unfold and tuck inside.

8

Repeat on all remaining sides.

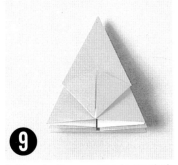

9

Fold up bottom corners to meet at the center.

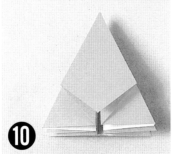

10

Unfold and fold inside using the creases just formed.

11

Repeat on all remaining sides.

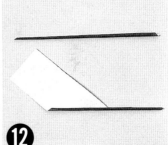

12

Cut 6" square paper into long quarters. Roll one strip tightly to form a handle.

13

Pierce a hole in the center of the shade. Insert handle through the hole and glue onto the peak.

14

Insert wire through the handle. Make a curve on one end.

15

Completed umbrella.

LITTLE PARTY PARTNERS

Colorful and unexpected shapes like these will please young guests. Start your party by letting them fold their favorite papers into their own containers. It will work well as an ice-breaker!

76 CANDY BOX

77 CANDY BOX WITH HANDLE

For instructions, see page 84.

78 DIVIDED BOX

For instructions, see page 85.

79 DIVIDED BOX WITH FRILLS

For instructions, see page 85.

1 Fold in half. Unfold and repeat to make crossing valley folds.

2 Bring all four corners to the center.

3 Turn over and bring all four corners again to the center.

4 Turn over and repeat to make an even smaller square.

5 Turn over. Lift center corners, open boxes, and press down outwards.

6 Repeat on all pockets.

7 Fold one flap in, three flaps under.

8 Turn over. Lift center corners.

9 Raise all corners and glue to the outside to reinforce.

10 Turn over for completed chair.

1 Begin with white side up. Fold in half and unfold; repeat to make valley folds crosswise. Turn over. Fold and unfold twice diagonally.

2 Press down using the creases.

3 With the center of paper towards you, fold upper edges to meet at the center.

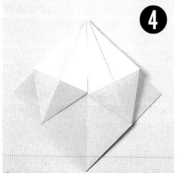

4 Open up pockets and press down to fold. Turn over and repeat.

5 Flip over and press tightly.

6 Fold upper edges to meet at the center.

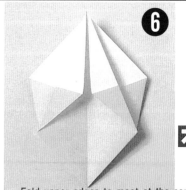

DIVIDED BOXES

Use 10"×10" paper

①

For both types of box, work steps ① - ④ in the same manner. Make crossing valley folds.

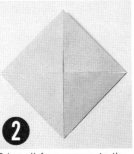

②

Bring all four corners to the center. (cushion fold)

③

Turn over and repeat.

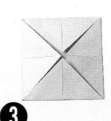

④

Fold in half twice to make crosswise creases. Unfold.

⑤

Turn over and open up pockets for completion.

To make frilled box

⑤

After step ④, turn over and fold in corners.

⑥

Fold down one side as if connecting side corners.

⑦

Unfold and repeat on the other side.

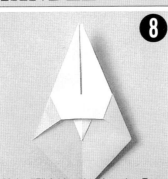

⑧

Repeat on remaining flaps.

⑨

Open up pockets for completed box.

CANDY BOX WITH HANDLE

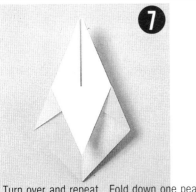

⑦

Turn over and repeat. Fold down one peak.

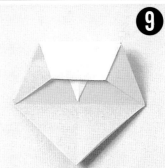

⑧

Make "Z" fold and tuck under. Turn over and repeat.

⑨

Repeat on all sides. Fold up bottom to make a crease.

⑩

Spread out for completed candy box.

To make handle

⑨

After step ⑧, fold up bottom to make a crease, leaving two peaks unfolded.

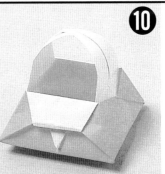

⑩

Spread out. Overlap tips of handles and glue together.

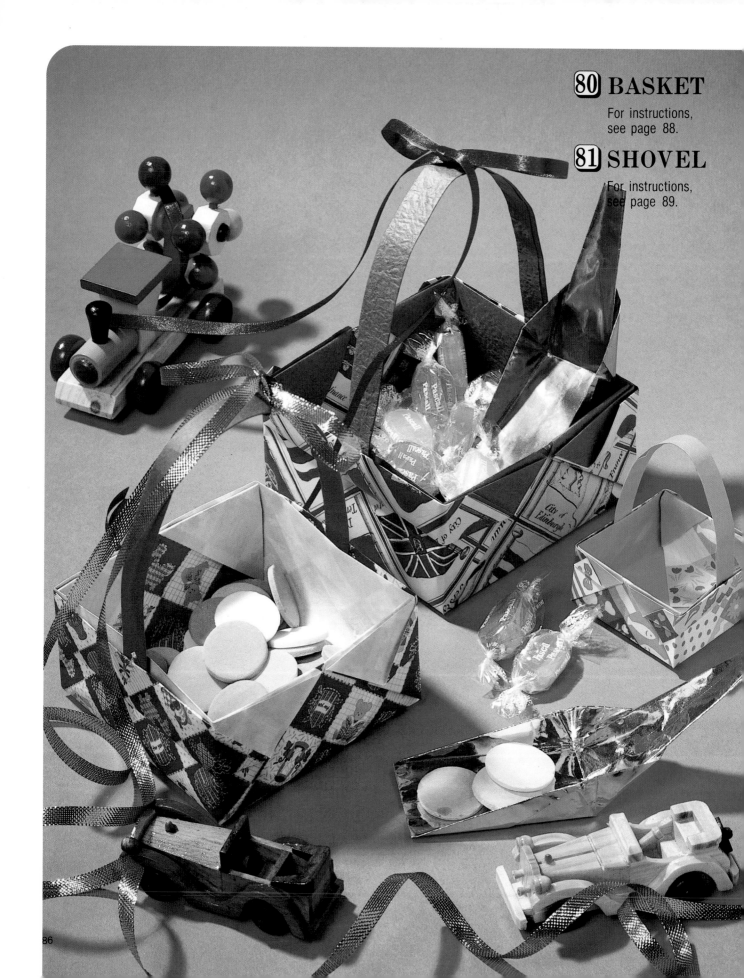

80 BASKET

For instructions,
see page 88.

81 SHOVEL

For instructions,
see page 89.

82 FLORAL CONTAINER
83 FLORAL COASTER

For instructions, see page 89.
This is a variation of TULIP (page 50).

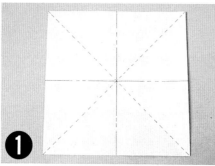

① Begin with colored side up. Fold in half and unfold; repeat to make valley folds crosswise. Turn over. Fold and unfold twice diagonally.

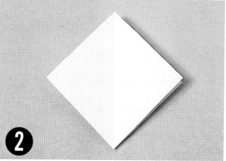

② Press down to fold along the creases.

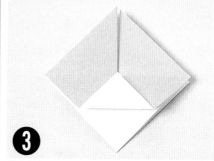

③ Fold down top corner to meet the bottom. Fold back half to make "Z" fold.

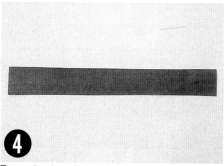

④ To make handle, cut out a strip of about 1½"×10".

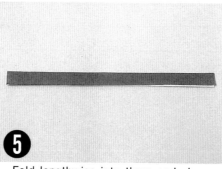

⑤ Fold lengthwise into three and glue.

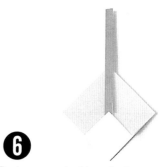

⑥ Tuck one end of handle into fold and glue to secure.

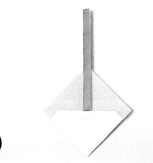

⑦ Fold up the flap in half.

⑧ Turn over and repeat to secure the handle.

⑨ Fold side corners under to match the center.

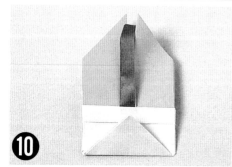

⑩ Turn over and repeat. Fold up bottom triangle to make a crease.

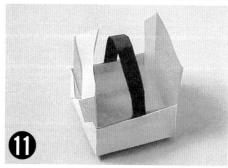

⑪ Spread out.

⑫ Fold the standing flaps into the box for completion.

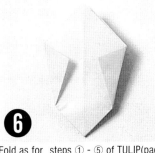

6 Fold as for steps ① - ⑤ of TULIP(page 52). Rotate ½ and fold in sides diagonally, not quite to the center. Fold up bottom to make a crease.

7 Unfold just once and open one flap. A small diamond is creased.

8 Push in the center crease from outside and make mountain fold through. Pressing down this fold to one side, fold the tip down.

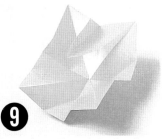

9 Press down through to the tip so as to line the bottom.

10 A pleat is formed in the center of one side.

11 Repeat on remaining corners and curl each "petals".

12 The size can be adjusted by altering the size and angle of folded triangles.

13 Completed container/coaster. For larger container, use 10"×10" paper.

SHOVEL

Use 6"×6" paper   **81** on page 86

1 Fold in half to make a crease. Unfold and bring sides to the center.

2 Fold up in half.

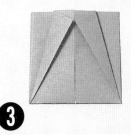

3 Fold upper corners to meet at the center.

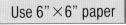

4 Turn over and fold sides to meet at the center.

5 Open up pockets and press down to fold from the center.

6 Fold in the sides of upper flap, overlapping each other.

7 Turn over and fold back top edge.

8 Pull down the top, and a shovel is formed. Refold bottom creases.

84 GIFTBOX

For instructions, see page 92.

85 EASY BOX

For instructions, see page 93.

1 Make a cushion fold: Fold in half twice and unfold. Bring all four corners to the center.

2 Fold top and bottom edges to align with the center.

3 Unfold and fold sides to center; unfold.

4 Pull top and bottom flaps out and refold the corners inwards.

5 Fold both flaps along the creases.

6 Completed box.

To make box

1 Make cushion fold as for lid.

2 Fold horizontally into $\frac{1}{3}$; unfold.

3 Fold vertically into $\frac{1}{3}$; unfold.

4 Turn over and fold to make a triangle, pressing only corners. Unfold and repeat on remaining corners.

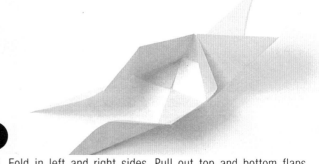

5 Unfold. Fold in left and right sides. Pull out top and bottom flaps. Refold the creases on the flap, pushing in corners.

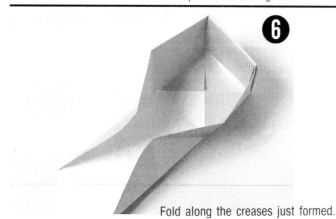

6 Fold along the creases just formed.

7 Repeat on the other flap for completion of box.

8 Completed giftbox.

NAME CARD HOLDER

1 Begin with CRANE base. Refer to page 48 for instructions.

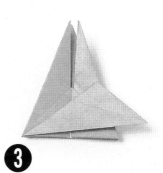

2 Bring up bottom tips by making inside folds, tucking into the sides of top half.

3 Fold down upper flap, leaving a little space from the bottom.

4 Repeat on the reverse side. Form head by making inside fold.

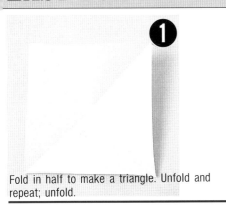

5 Press down the tail flat.

6 Fold in bottom corners of the tail. Press tightly.

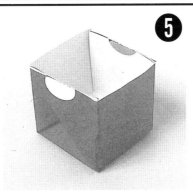

7 Completed card holder. Insert a card between wings and tail.

EASY BOX

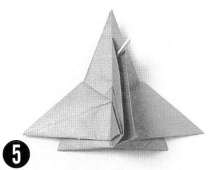

1 Fold in half to make a triangle. Unfold and repeat; unfold.

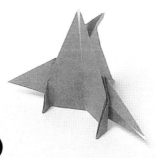

2 Make horizontal creases by folding into $\frac{1}{3}$.

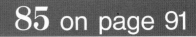

3 Make vertical creases as well.

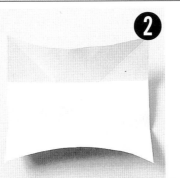

4 Pull up all four corners.

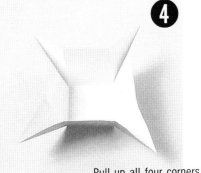

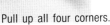

5

Note: Depth of the box can be adjusted by altering the position of creases made in steps ② and ③: For a shallow box, enlarge the center square.

Overlap two triangles on one side and secure the top with a sticker or staple. Repeat on the other side.

86 **PAPER DOILY**

For instructions, see page 96.

87 NAME CARD HOLDER

For instructions, see page 93.

88 SHELL GARLAND

For instructions, see page 96.

Jun

Mari

Ken

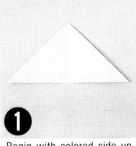

1 Begin with colored side up. Fold in half to make a triangle.

2 Fold in half again, matching right corner to left.

3 Fold in half again, this time folding one flap to the reverse side.

4 Bring the right side to align with the left, and fold back the tip. Flip to the right to mark on the side underneath.

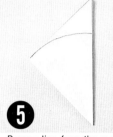

5 Draw a line from the marking so as to form a circle when unfolded.

88 on page 95

SHELL GARLAND
Use 3"×3" paper

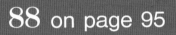

1 Fold in half. Make slits on the fold, at ¼" intervals.

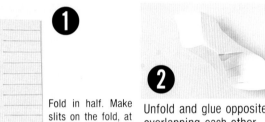

2 Unfold and glue opposite corners overlapping each other.

3 Overlap corners and glue white sides together so each side of the shell shows alternately.

6 Mark pattern and cut along the lines. Spread out for completed doily.

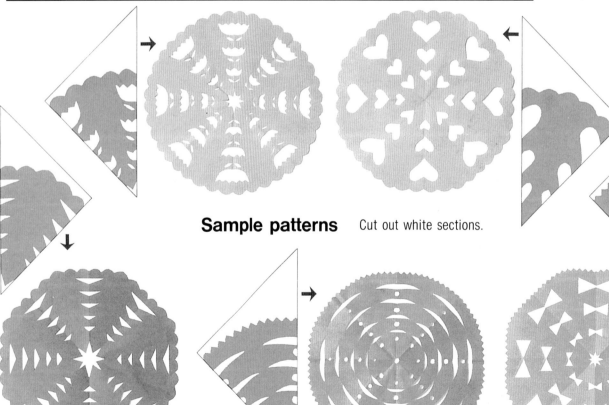

Sample patterns Cut out white sections.